STOLEN AIR

STOLEN AIR

SELECTED POEMS OF

OSIP MANDELSTAM

SELECTED AND TRANSLATED BY

CHRISTIAN WIMAN

INTRODUCTION BY ILYA KAMINSKY

AN *IMPRINT OF* HARPERCOLLINS*PUBLISHERS*

HarperCollins books may be purchased for educational, business, or sales promotional use. For information, please e-mail the Special Markets Department at SPsales@harpercollins.com.

FIRST EDITION

Designed by Mary Austin Speaker

Library of Congress Cataloging-in-Publication Data has been applied for.

ISBN 978-0-06-209942-6

22   OV/LSC   10 9 8 7 6

Возьми на радость из моих ладоней
Немного солнца и немного меда

Take, from my palms, for joy, for ease,
A little honey, a little sun

To exist is the artist's greatest pride. He desires no paradise other than being.

"The Morning of Acmeism"
1913

CONTENTS

VORONEZH NOTEBOOKS (1934–1937)

Secret Hearing: On Translating Osip Mandelstam

73

Notes and Acknowledgments

79

INTRODUCTION

OSIP MANDELSTAM: A LYRIC VOICE

by Ilya Kaminsky

When a great singer sings, the skin of space and of time go taut, . . . there is no corner left of silence or of innocence, the gown of life is turned inside out, the singer becomes earth and sky, time past and time to come are singing one of the songs of a single life.

—John Berger, *And Our Faces, My Heart, Brief as Photos*

And if the song's in search of earth, and if the song's
Ensouled, then everything vanishes
To void, and the stars by which it's known,
And the voice that lets it all be and be gone.

—Osip Mandelstam

"I have no manuscripts, no notebooks, no archives," wrote Osip Mandelstam. "I have no handwriting because I never write. I alone in Russia work from the voice, while all around the bitch-pack writes. What the hell kind of writer am I!? Get out you fools!"[1]

---

1 Osip Mandelstam, *The Prose of Osip Mandelstam: The Noise of Time, Theodosia, the Egyptian Stamp*, trans. Clarence Brown (Princeton, NJ: Princeton University Press, 1965).

To introduce such a voice, one must first ask: What is a lyric poet? And what is a lyric impulse? A lyric poet is a self-professed "instrument" of language who changes that language. And a lyric impulse? Well, that depends on the time and the circumstances. Here is Marina Tsvetaeva, a contemporary of Mandelstam's:

> My difficulty (in writing poems—and perhaps other people's difficulty in understanding them) is in the impossibility of my goal, for example, of using words to express a moan: ah—ah—ah. To express a sound using words, using meanings. So that the only thing left in the ears would be ah—ah—ah.[2]

•

January 3, 1891, Warsaw. To Emil and Flora Mandelstam, a boy is born.

> My father had absolutely no language; his speech was tongue-tie and languagelessness. The Russian speech of a Polish Jew? No. The speech of a German Jew? No again. Perhaps a special Kurland accent? I never heard such . . . speech . . . where normal words are intertwined with the ancient philosophical terms of Herder, Leibnitz, and Spinoza, the capricious syntax of a Talmudist, the artificial, not always finished sentence: it was anything in the world, but not a language, neither Russian nor German.[3]

2 Marina Tsvetaeva, *Poems of Marina Tsvetaeva*, trans. Jean Valentine and Ilya Kaminsky (forthcoming).
3 Osip Mandelstam, *Prose of Osip Mandelstam*.

The impossibility of my goal, for example, of using words to express a moan:
ah—ah—ah. To express a sound using words, using meanings.

•

When as a boy Osip Mandelstam brought his poems to a venerable journal of that time, the editor noted:

> Mandelstam did not feel the Russian language as his own;
> he observed it lovingly as if from a distance, finding its
> beauty . . . listening into it, flaming from mysterious victories over it. . . . The Russian language itself was beginning
> to sound new.[4]

I bring these testimonies not because they have to do with Mandelstam's father—and, to some extent, with the poet himself—being a non-native speaker of the Russian language. I bring them because I believe that no great lyric poet ever speaks in the "proper" language of his or her time. Emily Dickinson didn't write in "proper" English grammar but in *slant* music of fragmentary perception. Half a world and half a century away, César Vallejo placed three dots in the middle of the line, as if language itself were not enough, as if the poet's voice needed to leap from one image to another to make—to use T. S. Eliot's phrase—a raid on the inarticulate. Paul Celan wrote to his wife from Germany (a country he briefly visited during his voluntary exile in France): "The language with which I make my poems has nothing to do with one spoken here, or anywhere."

---

4 Sergei Makovskii, *Portrety Sovremenikov* (Portraits of Contemporaries) (New York: Chekhov Publishers, 1955).

But how to show this privacy of Mandelstam's Russian language while we discuss him in English? What is an English equivalent for this: "Pusti menya, otdai menya, Voronezh; / Uronish ty menya il' provoronish, / Te veronish menya ili vernesh, / Voronezh—blazh, Voronezh—voron, nosh." Reading these lines aloud (even without Russian), one cannot help but recall Gerard Manley Hopkins. The comparison with Hopkins also brings to mind Louise Bogan's claim that "many of the effects in Hopkins which we think of as triumphs of 'modern' compression are actually models of Greek compression, as transformed into English verse. . . ."[5] Substitute "Russian" for "English," and she comes close to describing Mandelstam. Here is what Mandelstam's Greek instructor remembers:

> He would be monstrously late for our lessons and completely shaken by the secrets of Greek grammar that had been revealed to him. He would wave his hands, run about the room and declaim the declensions and conjugations in a sing-song voice. The reading of Homer was transformed into a fabulous event; adverbs, enclitics, and pronouns hounded him in his sleep, and he entered into enigmatic personal relationships with them. . . . He arrived at the next lesson with a guilty smile and said, "I haven't prepared anything, but I've written a poem." And without taking off his overcoat, he began to recite. . . . He

---

5 Louise Bogan, *A Poet's Alphabet: Reflections on the Literary Art and Vocation* (New York: McGraw-Hill, 1970).

transformed grammar into poetry and declared that the more incomprehensible Homer was, the more beautiful. . . . Mandelstam did not learn Greek, he intuited it.[6]

•

He intuited it. From the inarticulate comes the new harmony. The lyric poet wakes up the language: the speech is revealed to us in a new unexpected syntax, in music, in ways of organizing the silences in the mouth. "You have no idea what kind of trash poetry comes from," Anna Akhmatova wrote of her own process.[7] From the very beginning of his literary life, the readers of Mandelstam recognized his ability to remake the Russian language. They said he saw Russia with a stranger's eyes. They said he wrote of an "imagined Russia."[8] They said, sometimes disparagingly, that he was lost in his "own language, his own Russian Latin."[9] But you could say this about any great lyric poet.

•

A few years after Osip's birth, in 1897, the Mandelstams move to St. Petersburg, where Osip's mother, Flora Osipovna, has "an almost manic need"[10] for relocating from one apartment to another. One wonders how this movement affected the poet,

6 Konstantin Mochulsky, *Vstrecha* 2 (1945).

7 Anna Akhmatova, *Collected Works*, 9 vols (Moscow: Ellis Lak Publishers, 1999).

8 Vladimir Markov, quoted in Clarence Brown, *Mandelstam* (Cambridge, Eng.: Cambridge University Press, 1973).

9 Ibid.

10 Nadezhda Mandelstam, *Hope Against Hope: A Memoir*, trans. Max Hayward (London: Collins and Harvill Press, 1971).

who later traveled all over the Soviet Union as if possessed, from Moscow to Kiev to Armenia to Crimea, looking for a home, an apartment, a room—and yet when the apartment was finally granted to him, later in life, no peace came:

I have lost my way in the sky—now, where?

•

Mandelstam's life is full of dualities, arguments, contradictions. A Jew born in Poland, he is Russian poetry's central figure in the twentieth century. A Modernist to the bone, he nonetheless believed in artistic (and ontological) unities and coherence. He wrote in rich, formal verse structures. Then sometimes he didn't. He rarely titled his poems. Sometimes he did. He kept more than one version of the same lyric and often inserted the same stanza into different poems. He composed aloud and recited to his wife, who wrote the poems down. Mandelstam was Russia's "most civilized poet," "a child of Europe,"[11] yet he found his "fullest breath"[12] not in worldly European capitals but in exile in the provincial town of Voronezh.

Perhaps such dualities and contradictions, too, lie at the heart of any modern poet's lyric impulse, which brings together the rawest opposites to produce that "divine harmony." But what is a lyric impulse in a time of war and revolution? Is it an individual voice? Can this voice speak for the nation? Can one person's voice speak of the epic events of his time? And can those events be channeled through a lyric voice?

---

11 George Ivask's statement.
12 Akhmatova, *Collected Works*.

In all this ocean of new rooms and suitcases, perhaps the only island was a bookshelf:

> The bookcase of early childhood is a person's lifetime companion. The disposition of its shelves, the selection of books, the color of the spines are perceived as the color, height, disposition of world literature itself.[13]

Or perhaps the island is the whole city: St. Petersburg, Petrograd, Piter, Leningrad—this "brother, Petropolis," the dying city, the city as a ship, the *Flying Dutchman*, around which his mother moves her furniture from one building to another, a city where he is brought as a Jew, the capital of the vast Slav empire. Here he writes his poetry, later to be called "Petersburgian," though he has defined the city as much as it him:

> You, with square windows,
> Squat houses in rows,
> Hello gentle,
> Hello winter,
> Petersburg, Petersburg,
> A thousand hellos.

What year is it? 1911. Mandelstam publishes his first poem. In St. Petersburg a group of young poets forms the Guild of Poets,

---

13 Osip Mandelstam, *Prose of Osip Mandelstam*.

naming themselves "craftsmen of the word." Nikolai Gumilyov is the "master" of this guild. His wife, Anna Akhmatova, is "secretary." Mandelstam becomes the Guild's "first violin."

They call William Shakespeare, François Villon, and François Rabelais their mentors, suggesting that Western European, not Russian, culture is their north star. As time will show, little unites their poetry except for a shared aim at precision. Mandelstam:

> Everything has become heavier and more massive; thus man must become harder, for he must be the hardest thing on earth; he must be to the earth what the diamond is to glass.

In 1912 they call themselves Acmeists.

•

Like St. Petersburg itself, Acmeism is a longing for clarity of architecture; it is a jump from darkness (of national poverty, of ignorance) that surrounds it; it is—as Mandelstam famously said—"a nostalgia for world culture."[14] Their opponents? The Symbolists. Yes, it is the old question of fathers and sons— Vasilli Gippus, a leading Symbolist poet, was Mandelstam's grade school teacher. Symbolists believed that the visible here and now was illusory and that everything is in any case fated to shatter or decompose—a prospect that filled them with fearful presentiment. In this world of visions, language is blurred. Opposed to this, the Acmeists demand "classical" precision of language, formal elegance:

---

14 Akhmatova, *Collected Works*.

One often hears: "That's fine and good, but it's yesterday." But I say: Yesterday has not yet been born. In reality, it hasn't even taken place yet. I want Ovid, Pushkin and Catullus all over again—I am not satisfied with the historical Ovid, Pushkin and Catullus.[15]

Mandelstam's first book—called, tellingly, *Stone*—appears in 1913. He is twenty-three years old. The Great War is about to begin. In three years he will meet Marina Tsvetaeva. In four years the Russian empire will fall.

•

And what happens around this little bubble in St. Petersburg, this little café where young poets meet, the Stray Dog? In Russia, Marc Chagall is emerging as a painter, Sergei Rachmaninoff and Igor Stravinsky are changing music, Constantin Stanislavski and Vsevolod Meyerhold are revolutionizing theater, Sergei Diaghilev is changing the classical Russian ballet.

And abroad, in France, Guillaume Apollinaire, inspired by Walt Whitman, is leading the same revolt against the French Symbolists. In London, Ezra Pound is swashbuckling through the tradition, taking what he wants, throwing out what he doesn't.

•

Yet a comparison with Pound or Apollinaire is misleading. Both American and French bards come on the heels of cen-

---

15 Osip Mandelstam, *Slovo I Kultura* (Moskow: Sov. Pisatel', 1987).

turies of poetic tradition. Mandelstam and his generation are the poets of the Silver Age of Russian literature. Alexander Pushkin, the father of the Russian poetic tradition, was the Golden Age.[16] And Pushkin died only a few decades before them.

And what was before Pushkin?

Darkness.

•

Pushkin:

Russia long remained alien to Europe. Accepting the light of Christianity from Byzantium, she participated in neither the political upheavals nor the intellectual activity of the Roman Catholic world. The great epoch of the Renaissance had no influence on her. . . . [Enslaved by Tatars] for two dark centuries only the clergy . . . preserved the pale sparks of Byzantine learning. . . . But the inner life of the enslaved people did not develop. The Tatars did not resemble the Moors. Having conquered Russia, they did not give it algebra or Aristotle.[17]

Russia had no history, according to Pyotr Chaadaev, the nineteenth-century public intellectual who left Russia and

---

16 Three well-known poets before Pushkin—Mikhail Lomonosov, Vasily Trediakovsky, and Gavrila Derzhavin—are universally accepted as minor compared to Pushkin. The beautiful and very moving early epic *Lay of Igor's Campaign* is only available in a nineteenth-century copy, but a number of scholars argue that it was actually written in the nineteenth century.

17 Alexander Pushkin, *The Critical Prose of Alexander Pushkin*, ed. and trans. Carl R. Proffer (Bloomington: Indiana University Press, 1969).

was either brave or crazy enough to return. But when Chaadaev declared this, he had overlooked language. Russia had no history and no literature, but it had its language. And soon enough Chaadaev's contemporaries, Pushkin and Nikolai Gogol among them, began to develop one of Europe's youngest—and fieriest—literary traditions.

•

This astonishing youth of Russian poetry is the true reason for Mandelstam's—and his generation's—"nostalgia for world culture." While Westerners such as Pound were looking elsewhere to *remake* the poetry of their time, the Russians, surrounded by centuries devoid of literature, looked to classics of other languages to *create* their country's poetic line. Leo Tolstoy and Fyodor Dostoevsky were able to write epics as late as the last half of the nineteenth century because there were no great epics in the language before then. Creating classics was a modern project for the Russians: it had the urgency of the time. Mandelstam:

> Classical poetry is perceived as *that which ought to be*, not that which has already been. . . . Contemporary poetry . . . is naïve. . . . Classical poetry is the poetry of revolution.[18]

•

1917. At the height of the Russian Revolution, Mandelstam, without much money,

18 Osip Mandelstam, *Slovo I Kultura*.

having by some miracle got a room at the Astoria (the most elegant hotel in St. Petersburg), took a tub bath several times each day, drank the milk that had been left at his door by mistake, and lunched at the Donon restaurant, where the proprietor, out of his mind, extended credit to everyone.[19]

What is the image of a lyric poet in a time of revolution? A young man taking baths several times a day and sipping milk while bombs explode outside his hotel room?

.

In a few months his best friend, the poet Nikolai Gumilyov, will be shot. Mandelstam will run from city to city for several years during the Civil War that follows the Revolution. He is imprisoned many times: Reds think that he (an intellectual) is a spy sent by the White Army; Whites think that he (a Jew) is one of the Communists.

In those days, "Mandelstam was always ardent and always hungry, but as everyone was hungry at the time, I should have said even hungrier than other people. . . . Once he called on us wearing a raincoat and nothing else. . . ."[20]

.

1919. Kiev. He marries Nadezhda. From this date until 1938 they are never apart. For years he and his new wife will walk

---

19 Arthur Lourié, Memoirs (Moscow, 1997).
20 Igor Stravinsky and Robert Craft, Retrospectives and Conclusion (New York: A. A. Knopf, 1969).

through the ruins of an empire, like a modern Don Quixote and Sancho Panza.

What are facts?

After the Revolution he applies to Maxim Gorky (through the Union of Poets) for a sweater and a pair of trousers. Gorky refused the trousers.[21]

•

Antonio Machado suggested: "In order to write poetry, you must first invent a poet who will write it." Whether Mandelstam was inventing himself or being forged by the pressure of his times, one thing is obvious: some of the best (and most joyful) writing comes in his darkest personal hours—hunger in Crimea, the restless life in Moscow, exile in Voronezh. "Restlessness was the first sign," Nadezhda wrote,

> that he was working on something and the second was the moving of his lips. . . . His head was twisted around so that his chin almost touched his shoulder; he was twirling his walking stick with one hand and resting the other on one of the stone steps to keep his balance. . . . When he was "composing" he always had a great need of movement. He either paced the room . . . or he kept going outside to walk the streets.[22]

And his view of the poetic vocation? Perhaps not surprisingly, it is rather close to that of his contemporary, W. H. Auden:

21 Nadezhda Mandelstam, *Hope Abandoned* (London: Harvill Press, 1974).
22 Nadezhda Mandelstam, *Hope Against Hope*.

Whatever its actual content and overt interest, every poem is rooted in imaginative awe. Poetry can do a hundred and one things, delight, sadden, disturb, amuse, instruct—it may express every possible shade of emotion, and describe every conceivable kind of event, but there is only one thing that all poetry must do; it must praise all it can for being as for happening.[23]

·

What is around him? The Russian empire is now the land of Five-Year Plans, with political purges, kolkhozes, starvation in the Ukraine (where he and Nadezhda were married). He is working at a journal, he writes children's books, he translates. He is falsely accused of stealing another's translation, and there follows an ugly public trial. He slaps the face of Alexei Tolstoy, *the red count*, the venerable novelist of that day. A scandal. He asks the secretary at Litfond (a financial foundation for supporting Soviet writers) about the costs of a coffin. Why? He doesn't want a coffin of his own; when he dies they can bury him without one. A scandal. He wants to be paid for his death up front.

·

Why repeat these anecdotes? *I live for two things in life* (said Akhmatova) *gossip and metaphysics.*

·

We tell these stories because we want an answer to the question: What is the lyric poet's response to the epic events of his

23 W. H. Auden, *Making, Knowing and Judging* (Oxford: Clarendon Press, 1956).

time? Here is Mandelstam's friend, Ilya Ehrenburg: "[P]oets greeted the Russian Revolution with wild shouts, hysterical tears, laments, enthusiastic frenzy, curses." Mandelstam "alone understood the pathos of the events, comprehended the scale of what was occurring."[24] And Joseph Brodsky: "His sense of measure and his irony were enough to acknowledge the epic quality of the whole undertaking. . . . Mandelstam's was perhaps the only sober response to the events which shook the world. . . ."[25]

Is this the same man who was sipping milk in the bath of the expensive hotel while all around him the city exploded?

We can't resolve his contradictions, but perhaps noting them can give us one way to speak about his lyric impulse.

•

Most twentieth-century Russian readers would have argued that the poet, any poet, *does* have a moral responsibility to his people. In that country, as a saying goes, a poet is a great deal more than just a poet. In pre-fifth-century Greece, "The Greeks always felt that a poet was in the broadest and deepest sense the educator of his people," that "the poet was still the undisputed leader of his people. . . ."[26] Many a Russian poet shared this feeling during the first twenty years of the twentieth century.

24 Osip Mandelstam, *Poems by Mandelstam*, trans. R. H. Morrison (London: Associated University Press, 1990).

25 Joseph Brodsky, *Less Than One: Selected Essays* (New York: Farrar, Straus & Giroux, 1986).

26 Werner Jaeger, *Paideia: The Ideals of Greek Culture* (New York: Oxford University Press, 1939).

But what does it mean to speak for one's people? And, just who *are* one's people?

.

When the government demands poems about collective farms, he writes about Greek myths. Later, when it demands patriotic songs for the working class, he writes an ode to "my necrotic, psychotic age." "I want to spit in the face of every writer who first obtains permission and then writes," he says. "I want to beat such writers over the head with a stick, . . . placing a glass of police tea before each one." And he thereby speaks for his people. In one single human voice. In a tone that is direct enough, playful enough, to be understood by his people.

He writes:

> [A]n heroic era has opened in the life of the word. The word is flesh and bread. It shares the fate of bread and flesh: suffering. People are hungry. The state is even hungrier. But there is something hungrier yet: time.

Such is a lyric poet's relationship to his time. He is both inside and outside of it; he suffers its immediate circumstances in the context of centuries. *The Noise of Time* (the title of his prose memoir) can also be translated as the hum of time, and humming was a part of this poet's writing process—almost as if the very substance of time were transformed within him, by means of him. "For an artist," Mandelstam wrote, "a worldview is a tool or a means, like a hammer in the hands of a mason, and the only reality is the work of art itself."[27]

•

While Akhmatova, in her *Requiem*, wrote what is probably the only lasting epic cycle of that time, Mandelstam offers us something entirely different: a voice singing outside of the people, a voice laughing, cursing, praising, asking for "a reader! an adviser! a doctor!" and waiting for the arrest, and jumping from a second-story window out of desperation, and asking a friend in the street for cash. It isn't the voice of a country. It is the voice of one human, a voice so naked in its feeling and rich in its Russian music that it now belongs to—and could be spoken by—anyone:

I have lost my way in the sky—now, where?

•

Why speak of him in quotations? Why fragments? "Destroy your manuscript," he wrote, "but save whatever you have written in the margins."[28]

•

Scholars rarely speak about the radical changes in his poetics over the years. Samuel Beckett, they say, decided to write in French because his English was getting "too good," too poetic. And Mandelstam? He begins as a shy Jewish boy writing in

27 Osip Mandelstam, *Prose of Osip Mandelstam*.
28 Ibid.

a "high-culture" voice, with numerous references to Homer, Ovid, et cetera. He ends, in the thirties, as a master of lyrics that mash together the high and the low, that are able to be surreal and down-to-earth at the same time. It is as if Alfred Lord Tennyson suddenly began to write like Emily Dickinson.

•

In April 1935 he writes one of his most humorous lyrics, "Mandelstam Lane." It is perhaps a minor poem, but one that would be unthinkable for early Mandelstam:

> What the hell sort of street is this?
> Mandelstam Lane.
> Diabolical name!
> Twist and twist
> And it all comes out the same:
> More kinked than the kinks in a madman's brain.
>
> Well, a ruler he was not.
> I'll say, and his morals hardly lily.
> And that's why this street,
> Or rut, really,
> Or pit pickaxed to the tune of Goddamn!—
> Goes by the name of Mandelstam.

•

Not long before this he reads his epigram to Stalin ("We Live") to a few friends, one of whom, it turns out, is an informer.

What are facts? Exile. Where he jumps from that window. A new exile, Voronezh. Where he writes his best poems. Return.

> He was a "Holy Fool," a iurodivyi of seventeenth-century Russia, a "bird of God" (he loved swallows and identified himself with the goldfinch); he was one of those imitators of Christ, God's fools, who were during Russia's times of troubles alone privileged to criticize the State. Like Ovid, he was an exile dreaming of Rome; like Dante, he wrote poems to "the measure and rhythm of walking." All poets were exiles, "for to speak means to be forever on the road."[29]

Yet another exile. Death in the camp. An unmarked grave.

·

And poems? After his death his poems were memorized by his wife and a few friends. They didn't keep originals in a written form. They wrote poems from memory, burned the paper, wrote poems from memory, burned the paper, wrote poems from memory, burned the paper. This continued for some decades.

This poetry belongs "to a select number of sacred texts which, like American Indian dream-poems but for more sinister reasons, were considered too momentous, too truthful, to write down."[30]

29 Osip Mandelstam, *Complete Poetry of Osip Emilevich Mandelstam*, trans. Burton Raffel and Alla Burago, introduction and notes by Sidney Monas (Albany: State University of New York Press, 1973).
30 These are D. M. Thomas's words on Akhmatova's work, but they could surely be applied to Mandelstam's poetry.

His wife, Nadezhda, will become an accomplished writer in her own right, publishing her moving, unforgettable memoir, *Hope Against Hope*, which instantly makes Mandelstam an international celebrity. And yet one is tempted to close this chapter where it began, with the words of Tsvetaeva, who, like Mandelstam, was forever opposed to any biographical explanations for the lyric voice:

> I do not know whether in general we need real-life interlinear translations for poetry: who lived, when, where, with whom, under what circumstances, etc., as in the high-school game familiar to everyone. The poetry has ground life up and cast it out, and out of the siftings that remain the biographer, who creeps after them practically on his knees, endeavors to recreate what actually happened. To what end? In order to bring us closer to the living poet. But surely he must know that the poet lives in *the poem. . . .*[31]

ON WIMAN'S VERSIONS

On Christian Wiman's versions and on translating without knowing the language, Mandelstam's own words come to mind:

> I experienced such joy in pronouncing sounds forbidden to Russian lips, mysterious sounds, outcast sounds, and perhaps, at some deep level, even shameful sounds.

---

31 Brown, *Mandelstam.*

There was some magnificent boiling water in a pewter teapot, and suddenly a pinch of black tea was tossed into it.

That's how I felt about the Armenian language.

Or this: In 1933 Mandelstam translated four poems by Petrarch into Russian. His biographer, Clarence Brown, writes:

> I had received the texts alone, with no indication of where the originals might be among Petrarch's hundreds of sonnets, so my first concern was naturally to seek these out. It was an awful headache. No sooner would I have identified this or that image in an opening line or two than some wild divergence would convince me that Mandelstam must have been working from another original. The 'other original' stubbornly refusing to turn up, I was driven back to my starting point, and had to conclude what is the point of this little narrative: that Mandelstam had translated Petrarch not into Russian, but into Mandelstam.[32]

•

A great poet deserves many translators:

> Each translator in turn produces a new translation, a new interpretation, a new form of expression in the other language. A poet's translators are complementary, not competitive. No translation from Mandelstam is a poem by Mandelstam.[33]

---

32 Osip Mandelstam, *Selected Poems*, trans. Clarence Brown and W. S. Merwin (New York: Atheneum, 1974).

33 Osip Mandelstam, *Poems by Mandelstam*.

Reading literature in translation, in a different language, in a different culture, often means that one is reading a complete invention, distant from the original, a myth.

This is particularly true of our understanding of Russian literature. Think of Constance Garnett's translations of Russian prose. Garnett translated every single nineteenth-century Russian author of some note and translated them all into English of the same tone, same modulation, same *everything*, in which Tolstoy and Dostoevsky became a sort of Tolstoevsky— with whom American readers of that time fell hopelessly in love.

This continued over much of the twentieth century and was even more true in the case of Russian poetry. Vladimir Nabokov was so frustrated by translations of Pushkin that his own literal version of *Onegin* contains hundreds and hundreds of footnotes. Brodsky would become apoplectic if you asked him about translations of Mandelstam or Akhmatova done by other hands in the seventies and eighties.

The patriotism and hurt pride of native speakers are touching but have very little to do with how literatures influence one another and how new gems grow from the myth and re-soundings of another literary tradition. By trying to bring something alien into English, we change English and broaden our own tradition. That is why reading works in translation is so important to us, why our language, since Geoffrey Chaucer, has thrived on translations, why (according to Pound) every new great age of English poetry is also a great age of translation.

Which brings us back to Wiman's versions of Mandelstam.

Why is this book important? Why, after at least a dozen other hands, do we need yet another version of this Russian Modernist in English?

Wiman mentions T. S. Eliot's sense of the "auditory imagination," and indeed evidence of an auditory imagination is all over these pages. "[A] poet hears rhythms before he has words for them," Wiman says. Yes. One thinks of Mandelstam's belief that "What distinguishes poetry . . . is that it rouses us, and shakes us awake in the middle of the word. Then the word turns out to be far longer than we thought."[34]

Brodsky said that in his exile in Siberia he translated Auden by copying the first line via a word-by-word dictionary version and imagining what the rest of the poem was like based purely on its sounds. Of course, this isn't new in the English tradition—any interested parties should consult Louis and Celia Zukovsky's *Catullus* for an example of translating poetry by ear alone. What is new and extremely interesting about Wiman's versions is that tone and content *do* get through here. No matter how different the words may be in Wiman's hunt for the musical equivalent in English, the essence of Mandelstam's originals seems to survive. This is the sort of English translation that Brodsky hoped for—and that everyone else, for decades, thought impossible.

•

A case study: I shared Wiman's version with an American poet, who wondered: "But why all this alliteration? I bet it's not in

---

34 Osip Mandelstam, *Conversation About Dante*, trans. Jane Gary Harris (Ann Arbor, Michigan: Ardis, 1979).

the original!" But it is, and very much so. Just sound out the lines I quoted earlier, which are not at all anomalous:

> Pusti menya, otdai menya, Voronezh;
> Uronish ty menya il' provoronish,
> Te veronish menya ili vernesh,
> Voronezh—blazh, Voronezh—voron, nosh.

As I mentioned, Bogan argued, rather persuasively, that Hopkins was influenced by Greek grammar. What might be done in English if Russian ways of alliteration and rhyme are introduced, one wonders? This was largely Brodsky's experiment, and his criticism of other translators of Mandelstam always centered on sound or the lack thereof. Wiman's versions seek to meet Mandelstam at this fundamental level.

•

And the result? Gorgeous poetry in English, first of all:

> My animal, my age, ravenous in your cage,
> What flute might bend the bars, bind the gnarled
> Knees of days?. . .

This whole book is "A lullaby for human grief, / Of human grief," a song that is very much flesh and bone of Wiman's native English and yet, miraculously, also a fairly close translation of Osip Mandelstam. When I say "fairly close translation," I am thinking particularly of pieces like "The Necklace" or "Hard Night," which have an almost word-by-word correspondence to the originals *and* a stunning—and a very "Mandelstamian"—music.

Then there are the poems whose forms veer away from the originals but whose tones are, I believe, still quite faithful: "You," for instance, with the lovely opening that I have already quoted, which leads us into that city that Dostoevsky said was the expression of a madness that didn't know that it was mad, St. Petersburg, suddenly alive again, in English. At other moments, entire traditions merge, as when, in "Night Piece," Christopher Marlowe marries Mandelstam:

Come love let us sit together
In the cramped kitchen breathing kerosene.

For me, these moments are among the most interesting, because something unexpected is born when one poet abandons the ego and enters the world of another but does so on his own terms, in his own language. Also particularly memorable are the poems in which Wiman takes on the more humorous, more reckless side of Mandelstam, poems such as "Bootleg Love Song" and "Herzoverse." This side of Mandelstam, though it's very much a part of his middle and late work, is not well known to English readers, who are accustomed to the famous elegiac tones ("Tristia") or the caustic civic voice ("We Live"). Wiman is certainly having fun in these lighter poems, making up words (as did Mandelstam) and cutting or adding lines as necessary. And yet somehow, once again, he gets the *tone* of the Russian, while creating entirely new poems in English.

Of course, not everything here is translation or even close—as Wiman is the first to admit. This is not because he is unable to do a good version from the word-by-word trot, but because he is interested in making poems that are alive and relevant to our moment. He is also perfectly willing to give other translators credit where it is due, thus the phrase "Today Is All Beak" from W. S. Merwin's earlier translation (a phrase that does not, in fact, exist in Mandelstam) migrates here—or rather, we see here what else can be done with these four words if one decides to take this poem in a slightly different direction. One finds other influences, too. Catullus, for example ("Shut up: to be alone is to be alive"), whom Mandelstam loved. And Hopkins, of course, who is everywhere (in fact, I think that in these versions Wiman comes closer to Hopkins than any other living American poet). And then, again—wonderfully—there is Mandelstam himself, sounding for a moment exactly as he would have if he had written in English:

Forgive me this, forgive what I am saying.
Whisper it, less than whisper, like someone praying.

•

Jorge Luis Borges's piece "Pierre Menard, Author of the Quixote" is about a twentieth-century author who attempts to go beyond a "mere" translation of Don Quixote by trying to "re-create" it, line by line, in the original seventeenth-century Spanish. Written shortly after Borges's own attempt at translation, this piece is perhaps the most apt metaphor for this clearly insane act: the literary translation.

Why, then, do it? Speaking about Mandelstam's great translator, Paul Celan (who also took enormous liberties with the originals), John Felstiner observed that for Celan poetry itself had to do with speaking to, and reaching out toward, another poet and person (one thinks of Mandelstam asking for "a reader! an adviser! a doctor!"). It's the desperate—and sometimes rescuing—message in a bottle (an image Celan drew, in fact, from Mandelstam). For Celan, this relationship was a kind of handshake, a reaching across space and time. "When [Celan] says, the poem reaches toward another, over-against, an addressable Thou, you can also hear him saying this about a poet reaching out to the translator. . . . Ultimately, at its finest, Celan saw something redemptive about the act of translation."[35]

Though Wiman in his translator's note quite honestly admits the distance between himself and Mandelstam, as I was reading these poems I kept thinking of Nabokov's first novel in English, *The Real Life of Sebastian Knight*, the last paragraph of which I reproduce here, with a few minor changes. To my mind, this paragraph articulates not only something crucial about Wiman's relation to Mandelstam (as I see it) but also something about the act of translation itself, perhaps even the act—the drama—of reading any poetry with our full selves:

So, I did not see [M.] after all, or at least I did not see him alive. But those few minutes I spent listening to what I thought was his breathing changed my life as completely as

35 Ilya Kaminsky, "Attentiveness—Natural Prayer of the Soul: Interview with John Felstiner," *In Posse Review*, http://www.webdelsol.com/InPosse/kaminsky-felstiner12.htm (accessed August 18, 2011).

it would have been changed, had [M.] spoken to me before dying. Whatever his secret was, I have learnt one secret too, and namely: that the soul is but a manner of being—not a constant state—that any soul may be yours, if you find and follow its undulations. The hereafter may be the full ability of consciously living in any chosen soul, in any number of souls, all of them unconscious of their interchangeable burden. Thus—I am [M.] I feel as if I were impersonating him on a lighted stage, with the people he knew coming and going—the dim figures of the few friends he had, the scholar, and the poet, and the painter,—smoothly and noiselessly paying their graceful tribute. . . . They move round [M.]—round me who am acting [M.],—and the old conjuror waits in the wings with his hidden rabbit; and [N.] sits on a table in the brightest corner of the stage. . . . And then the masquerade draws to a close. The bald little prompter shuts his book, as the light fades gently. The end, the end. They all go back to their everyday life . . . —but the hero remains, for, try as I may, I cannot get out of my part: [M.]'s mask clings to my face, the likeness will not be washed off. I am [M.], or [M.] is I, or perhaps we both are someone whom neither of us knows.[36]

36 Vladimir Nabokov, *The Real Life of Sebastian Knight* (Norfolk, Conn: New Directions, 1941).

EARLY POEMS

(1910–1925)

CATHEDRAL, EMPTY

When light, failing,
Falling

Through stained glass,
Liquefies

The long grass
At the feet of christ,

I crawl diabolical
To the foot of the cross

To sip the infinite
Tenderness

Distilled
From destroyed

Hearts:
An air of thriving

Hopelessness
Like a lone cypress

Holding on
To some airless

Annihilating height.

(1910)

CASINO

Pointless any happiness that happens by plan:
To live in nature is to suffer luck.
Thus blessed, thus cursed, I am myself again,
Empty-tipsy, drinking to the lees my lack.

Wind-tousled cloud, cloud-tousled chance,
Deep in the unseen an anchor drops, and clings.
O my lilting, my light-sheer, my linen existence:
As of another nothing floating over things.

I like the cakelike casino on the dunes,
And how the strict fingers of skeletal light
Come alive on the baize, and the view, vast as mist.

I like the tone of green that oceans in,
And the tight rosebuds of wine that bloom in the mind,
And the towering, scouring seagull, in whose eyes nothing is
    lost.

(1912)

BRING ME TO THE BRINK

Bring me to the brink of mountains, mystic
Dread, rapture of fear I feel and . . . fail.
Still: the swallow slicing blue is beautiful.
Still: the cloud-tugged bell tower's frozen music.

There is in me a man alive, a man alone,
Who, heart-stopped above a deep abyss,
Can hear a snowball grow one snowflake less,
The clock-tick accretions of dust becoming stone.

No. I am not that man, not that sadness
With its precise ice, its exquisite rue.
The pain that sings in me does not sing, and is true.

O whirlwind, O real wind
In which the avalanche is happening,
All my soul is bells, which will not ring.

(1912)

NIGHT SONG

The bread is blight and the air's acetylene,
Wounds impossible to doctor.
Joseph, by his own blood bartered
Off to Egypt, grieved for home no harder.

Unslaked sky. Sleetlight of stars.
And the stallioned Bedouins, avatars
Of the day's vagueness, and the pain
Of vagueness, close their eyes and improvise

Out of nothing more than the mist
Of events through which they've passed:
Coarse wind, a horse traded for grain, small wars
With sand in which an arrow was lost.

And if the song's in search of earth, and if the song's
Ensouled, then everything vanishes
To void, and the stars by which it's known,
And the voice that lets it all be and be gone.

(1913)

LET CITIES SUBSIDE TO THEIR NAMES

Let cities subside to their names,
Brief meanings that flare in the ear:
Washington, London, Moscow, Rome:
Existence is our home, and is here.

Let presidents rule what they can.
Let preachers have their narrow door.
Houses and altars hallowed of man
Are houses and altars, no more.

(1914)

HARD NIGHT

Hard night. Homer. Homeless sails.
I've listened to the list of ships in my own voice.
I've seen, as my own voice fails,
Those strange cranes arrowing sorrowing over Hellas.

Ever alien, ever more interior, these shores,
And the sun-flecked, god-picked wings glinting spray—
Anxiety's army, ghost souls of Achaea,
Without your one longing, what is dying for?

The singer and the sea, all things are moved by love.
But what is that to me? Homer is dead.
And a wall of silence, eerily eloquent,
Breaks like a black wave above my bed.

(1915)

TRISTIA

There is, I know, a science of separation
In night's disheveled elegies, stifled laments,
The clockwork oxen jaws, the tense anticipation
As the city's vigil nears its sun and end.
I honor the natural ritual of the rooster's cry,
The moment when, red-eyed from weeping, sleepless
Once again, someone hoists the journey's burden,
And to weep and to sing become the same quicksilver verb.

But who can prophesy in the word *good-bye*
The abyss of loss into which we fall;
Or what, when the dawn fires burn in the Acropolis,
The rooster's rusty clamor means for us;
Or why, when some new life floods the cut sky,
And the barn-warm oxen slowly eat each instant,
The rooster, harbinger of the one true life,
Beats his blazing wings on the city wall?

I love the calm and custom of quick fingers weaving,
The shuttle's buzz and hum, the spindle's bees.
And look—arriving or leaving, spun from down,
Some barefoot Delia barely touching the ground . . .
What rot has reached the very root of us
That we should have no language for our praise?
What is, was; what was, will be again; and our whole lives'
Sweetness lies in these meetings that we recognize.

Soothsayer, truth-sayer, morning's mortal girl,
Lose your gaze again in the melting wax
That whitens and tightens like the stretched pelt of a
    squirrel
And find the fates that will in time find us.
In clashes of bronze, flashes of consciousness,
Men live, called and pulled by a world of shades.
But women—all fluent spirit; piercing, pliable eye—
Wax toward one existence, and divining they die.

(1918)

THE NECKLACE

Take, from my palms, for joy, for ease,
A little honey, a little sun,
That we may obey Persephone's bees.

You can't untie a boat unmoored.
Fur-shod shadows can't be heard,
Nor terror, in this life, mastered.

Love, what's left for us, and of us, is this
Living remnant, loving revenant, brief kiss
Like a bee flying completed dying hiveless

To find in the forest's heart a home,
Night's never-ending hum,
Thriving on meadowsweet, mint, and time.

Take, for all that is good, for all that is gone,
That it may lie rough and real against your collarbone,
This string of bees, that once turned honey into sun.

(NOVEMBER 1920)

MY ANIMAL, MY AGE

My animal, my age, who alive can gaze
Into those eyes without becoming you?
Who alone can use, like a kind of sacrificial glue,
Word and blood to bind and mend these centuries?

Blood the builder brings forth the future
From the garroted throat of this very hour.
Meanwhile, some worm, some parasite of power,
Slime to the tip of his larval lips, licks them.

.

All creatures touched to life, clutched
By life, are the beings they must be and bear.
Mindlight, spinelight, and somewhere, nowhere,
The dark wave . . .

.

Blood the builder brings forth the future.
From the throat of nature
Blood the builder bleeds and sings
And like a fish on fire your life lands
On the hot sands of some far shore
While from a mortared sky
Blood the builder pours
And pours indifference over your final why.

·

My animal, my age, ravenous in your cage,
What flute might bend the bars, bind the gnarled
Knees of days, and bring forth a world
Of newness, world trued to music—
A lullaby for human grief,
Of human grief,
While the adder breathes in time in the grass.

·

Wave after wave of grave aboriginal green,
And then, buds plumped to the point of bursting,
And then, again, all the soft detonations of simple
    spring . . .

But not for you, my beautiful, my pitiful,
My necrotic, psychotic age.
More cruel for the weakness that taunts you,
More crippled for the supple animal that haunts you,
You stagger on,
Staring back at the way you've taken:
Mad tracks in a land called Gone.

(1923)

YOU

You, with square windows,
Squat houses in rows,
Hello gentle,
Hello winter,
Petersburg, Petersburg,
A thousand hellos.

•

To stick in the instant
Like a fish,
Like a dead fish,
Like winter-picked ribs

That up through the ice
Upset the blades;
To sing flinging
Skates down skate-cluttered hallways . . .

•

Once upon a time
In a time still near
A potter and his fire
Floated like a tiny pyre
Farther and farther
On the red-shadowed water.

Tested by darkness,
Wrested from darkness,
A simple cup,
A plain well-made plate,
Sold on the stone stoop
Of any street.

·

Walk, work boots.
Get going, goners.
Past the Guest Yard,
The fields packed hard,

Where the ripe mandarin
Peels itself for your pleasure
And a measure of coffee
Crackles ecstatic

In your hands,
Smuggled from the cold
And ground to golden,
Home.

·

Chocolate chocolate
Brick brick
House house
Sweet Petersburg!
Nuzzleblizzard.

.

And the living rooms
With their pulseless silence,
All the unplunked pianos,
Sunken chairs, mingled airs
Of science and séance
As the doctors are treating people
—or maybe feeding people?—
With the *Neva*'s deathless prose . . .

.

After the bath,
After the opera,
After the after,

It's all the same,
Whoever one was,
Wherever one goes,

_____

Neva is a literary journal based in St. Petersburg.

The cluelessness
And the youlessness
As the last tram

Lets one in,
So warm the eyes
So easily close . . .

(1925)

THE MOSCOW NOTEBOOKS

(1930–1934)

INTERROGATION

Official paper, officious jowls, unswallowable smells
Of vomit, vodka, cells, bowels,
And all these red-tape tapeworms gorging on reports.

Choir, stars, your highest, your holiest silences . . .
But first, sign here on the dotted line
That they may grant you permission to shine.

(OCTOBER 1930)

NOT ONE WORD

Not one word.
Purge the mind of what the eye has seen:
Woman, prison, bird.
Everything.

Otherwise some wrong dawn
Your mouth moves
And a sudden pine
Needles through your nerves,

A trapped wasp crazes
In your brain,
And in the old desk's ink stain
A forest mazes

Inward and inward
To the unpicked
And sun-perfected
Blueberries

Where you now and now always
Must stand,
An infinite inch
Between that sweetness

And your hand.

(OCTOBER 1930)

THE PEOPLE HOWL, THE BEASTS SPEAK

The people howl, the beasts speak,
And the splendid official, who on a lark

Hopped a daytime train without his papers,
Now pickaxes ice with a quiet tribe of lepers.

Taste it, that last glass of Black Sea wine he sipped like
    freedom
In the dreamreeking tavern on the road to Erzurum.

(NOVEMBER 1930)

LENINGRAD

I have come back to my city, so known my very being weeps:
Old illness, old comforts, gauzy dreams, swollen sleeps.

Now, now, child, little one, take your medicine, drink it down:
A little sip of fish oil from the streetlamps that light this dark
    town.

Look alive: it's December, remember how near you are
To night: already the yolk of light marred with toxic tar.

Petersburg! I don't want to die.
I watch my telephone with a watched eye.

Petersburg! I know every floor, every door the dead
Do not answer: one by one they open in my head.

I have come back to my city, quietly, so quietly,
But the doorbell's wired to my nerves, rooted in the meat of
    me,

And all night I itch untouchable, as with a paraplegic's pains,
Waiting for the door to rattle in its chains.

(DECEMBER 1930)

POWER

I was a child in the churning world,
Flinching at the unflinching sentries,
Terrified of the all-eyed oysters.

Nothing in me, if I was in me, wanted that.

To pose under a portico in a nimbus
Of self and with a dead animal for a hat,
To hear the minksqueaking pitter-pat of a little gypsy girl,
Her firelithe body eating money by the lemon river.

A child could feel it, the age's blade being sharpened . . .

And so I learned, and painfully earned, on the beaches of the
    Black Sea,
The European allure of sorrow
Sensualized in quotations, flirtations, some random clavicle
Cutting through me like a scalpel.

A man returned, or almost . . .

Petersburg, pitiless city,
With your fire-scarred towers and frostburned poor,
Your insolent adolescence,
your furious frivolous doom,

What ancient claim do you make on me?

A child enchanted by a moonskin nude
Astride a storybook stallion cries out her name
To a man muttering through old streets near dawn
Godiva, good-bye Godiva, Godiva Godiva gone . . .

(JANUARY 1931)

NIGHT PIECE

Come love let us sit together
In the cramped kitchen breathing kerosene.
There's fuel enough to forget the weather,
The knife is ours and the bread is clean.

Come love let us play the game
Of what to take and when to run,
Of come with me and come what may
And holding hands to hold off the sun.

(JANUARY 1931)

PRAYER

Help me, Lord, this night my life to save.
Hold me, Lord, your servant, your slave.
Hear me, O Lord, alive in Petersburg, my grave.

(JANUARY 1931)

BOOTLEG LOVE SONG

I will tell you with one divine
Apocalyptic belch:
It's all Being's screech, bootleg hooch,
Angel mine.

For the lean Hellenes Helen topless
Topped the sky.
For ossified Osip
Some vulgar Hulga highballs Nehi.

Wine-dark the waves, sun-shellacked
The Greeks, and Beauty plucked
Like a grape.
For me: drymouth, and hangover's daylong gape.

Ah the kisslessness
Of emptiness,
And the fall you finally know is true,
When even destitution doesn't want you.

Slag-digger, slug-bugger, booger-sugar,
It's all the same damn slog.
O Mary, rumwarm mother of us,
Glug grog.

I will tell you with one divine
Apocalyptic belch:
It's all Being's screech, bootleg hooch,
Angel mine.

(MARCH 1931)

HERZOVERSE

Once upon a time there lived a Jew,
A musical Jew, I tell you,
Named Alexander Herzowitz.
Sweet as sherbet, his Schubert,
A jewel, I tell you, a musical jewel,

Dawn to dusk, day after day,
The same damn jewel in the same damn way:
What is this, Salamander Slivovitz,
Insanity's sonata?
And what are you, a holy fool?

Scherzowitz! Enoughofits!
Let the *dulce de leche* maiden
Swoon Schubert through her skin,
Let the children's sleigh allegro
This swiftness and darkness and starsparkle snow.

We're not afraid to die,
You and I,
To flutter down like a dove, a musical dove,
To hang on a black hook like a coat and glove,
A worn, one-armed coat and a tattered, three-fingered glove.

O maestro, Alexander Herzowitz,
Whose hands and heart are blown to bits,

What in you pins you there,
My lonely mister, heaven's busker,
Playing your sad, your same, your only air?

(MARCH 27, 1931)

GODNAUSEA

By torchlight burning bewildered with purpose
Into the cellar of the six-toed untruth:
Well, my pretty, she says,
Lifting the hairy turnip of her head:
Are you hungry, or are you dead?

She sighs like a vent in earth,
Slicing pickled mushrooms with old men's faces,
Ladling out a gloopy tuberous stew
Of afterbirth.

A heave of hot air, heaving floor,
But the door is indivisible dirt,
Aswarm with worms.
Eat, eat . . . there's always more.

Lice in moss, nice and quiet, really,
And the light's motes such pretty little flies—
Sing us the old lullaby of alibis,
Sugarmonster, bugmother, me . . .

(APRIL 1, 1951)

A TOAST

I drink to the tasseled shoulders of the tall top brass
And the frigid rich wrapped in animal.

To the wheeze and laze of asthmatic days,
To Petersburg spleen, I lift my glass.

I drink to the toss and gossip of Savoy pine trees,
Oils of unlikeness in Parisian galleries,

Exhaust on the Champs-Elysées,
Debutante waves on the Bay of Biscay.

To choice roses chucked from Rolls-Royces,
Plump jugs of spanking Alpine cream,

Pink English ladies bestowing scorn,
Malarial tom-toms tamed with quinine.

To all this, and to more,
To all that they have reproached me for,

I propose a toast—
And yet, I am not quite sure which will do—

An Asti Spumante's happy frost
Or an aged Châteauneuf-du-Pape,

With its afternotes of nuts and rue.

(APRIL 11, 1931)

GOWN OF IRON

Hold hard my word-hoard, wound-cured, forever's breath.
Seek in song's quicksilvering circles harsh conscience, stark
    patience, bitter tar of work.

In Novgorod, let no-God be the name of the blackest well,
    that the sweetness extracted may be absolute, and anyone's.
In time, in harm, who knows, sharp in that heavened eye the
    seven-tipped star of Bethlehem might shine.

Father, friend, O my cold counselor, I, lonely prodigal,
    lopped-off limb of the human tree,
Do hereby promise to plane the wood that is given me, and to
    plumb the lines, and to polish the grain of a frame
Fit for neo-Tartars to waterboard our latter kingdom's quislings.

Oh, if only, if even a little, if even a little they loved me, the
    torturer's tools . . .

Red rover, red rover, cry all the hell-tanned martyrs, *let Osip come
    over* . . .

So I come running dreaming frozen in the gown of iron that
    is my life,
To find, in the old forest, the old and moldering ax,
And hear, like a melon so plump-ripe its rind leaps ahead of
    the knife, the crisp wet crack of a severed neck.

(MAY 3, 1931)

LET FLY THE WILD

Fuck this sulk, these pansy stanzas tickling doom.
Devil me down to the roots of my hair,
And further—ah, François, le barbier débonnaire,
Scalp me back to the Paris of youth!

Odds are I'm alive.
Odds are, like a jockey gone to slop,
There's skip and nimble in me yet,
There's a length of neck to stake, and there's cunning,
And there's an animal under me running
Which, if I can hold on, will not stop.

Thirty-one years alive in cherry white,
Thirty-one years belong to blossoms.
Who hears them, the earthworms like jellied rain
Chewing through soil and the solid dead
While all of tall-sailed Moscow whips and snaps
In the instant's wind?

Easy, boy: impatience, too, is candy,
And we are sulk-soft, silk-kneed, mild.
Let's take the track early, and pace ourselves,
Until all the trapped acids trickle out as sweat,
And we take time between our teeth like a bit
And let fly the wild.

(JUNE 7, 1931)

BATYUSHKOV

Vegetable sage, wizard of indolence,
My tender friend strides the alleyways
Inhaling the souls of roses
Like a man alive and singing *Zafna!*

There is, it seems, no heresy like the heresy
Of saying good-bye . . .
So I bow, and give his pale cold glove a squeeze—
With, I admit, a little friendly envy.

He smirks. *I am beholden to thee*
I say like a Quaker, and freeze
Suddenly, on stilts in a sea of jelly.
Never again that ease

With awkwardness, tsunami
Of suffering, of sumptuousness,
Creation's spell, brotherhood's bell,
Our very selves showering down on us.

I've lost my taste for praise,
He says with a little pirouette of silhouette.
Only the slashing accident,
The peeled-grape feel of real poetry . . .

Konstantine Nikolaevich Batyushkov (1787–1855) is one of the most famous and
influential Russian poets. *Zafna* is the name of a woman in his poem "The Spring."

Batyushkov! I can still hear the tick tick
Of your walking stick
Wanding bricks to pigeons
And pigeons back to bricks.

Batyushkov! I can still feel,
Recalling your shabby, shambling back,
Love, like a piece of my soul
I never knew I lacked.

(JUNE 18, 1932)

TO THE TRANSLATOR

Forget it. Don't tempt yourself with tongues
Whose blood is not your own.
Better to bite a lightbulb, eat an urn.

How long the haunting, how high the cost, that sky-wide
    scream
Of the bird we cannot name—
Like a happy man undone by an alley-flash of lace.

In the end, when the soul rends a man toward that timelessness
It was his whole ambition to express,
To speak a denatured thing is to fling the first dirt on your
    own cold face.

Happy Tasso, bittersweet Ariosto, how they enchant us,
    enchant us,
Until they don't. And if it's they who come, in the hour of ice,
Throbbing their blue-brained truths, their starved and larval
    eyes?

So: you, then. Your animal urge. Your primal pride.
To you is given this sponge dipped in vinegar, bitter wad
Of silence: you, who thought love of sound alone could lead
    to God.

(1933)

FLAT

Now you've got a flat you can write poetry.

—BORIS PASTERNAK

The flat is quiet as paper,
Stripped of keepsakes and of schemes;
Walls so thin you hear your neighbor gargle,
And some, their neighbor's dreams.

All our affairs are in order.
The phone squats like a watched frog.
All our traveling rags and tatters
Travel still in stillness, like fog.

Even the radiator gives a start,
Though there's nowhere left to run,
And dissembling is my highest art,
Virtuoso of the comb and clucking tongue.

Ruder than a Komsomol cell,
Cruder than the students' chanted plan,
I teach an executioner how to kill
By teaching birdsongs to a man.

Ration books are all I read,
Loudspeaker speeches all I hear.
Listen: even a lullaby can bleed.
Learn, little kulak child, to fear.

Some realist neo-ruralist hack,
Some sheep-shit worm of a collective farm,
Some ink-bleeding, praise-needing party flack—
Deserves just this kind of calm.

Soon enough, when the last purge has boiled
All but salt from the public pot,
Some family man, some salt-of-the-earth old soul,
Will see this moth of me, and swat.

Oh, the malice of mildness, these thumbscrew thank-yous,
The devil's poetry of politesse:
As though right through these flimsy walls and windows
Dead Nekrasov himself still hammered us.

Believe me, it won't be sweet Hippocrene
That roars through these walls in the end,
Though it will be ancient, and sudden,
And will completely possess us, my friend.

(NOVEMBER 1933)

The epigraph is not in the original, but Pasternak's remark did precipitate
this poem. **Komsomol**: a Soviet youth organization linked to the Communist
Party. **Kulak**: a prosperous peasant; after the revolution, they were system-
atically destroyed as a social class. **Nekrasov**: a civic, social poet from the
nineteenth century. **Hippocrene**: in classical mythology, a fountain on Mount
Helicon and the source of poetic inspiration.

WE LIVE

We live, and love, but our lives drift like mist over what we love.
Two steps we are a whisper; ten, gone.

Still, we gather, we gossip, we laugh like humans,
And just like that our Kremlin gremlin comes alive:

His grubworm clutch, all oil and vile,
His deadweight deadwords, blonk blonk.

Listen: his jackhammering jackboots: even the chandelier shakes.
Look: a hairy cockroach crawls along his grin

At the cluck-cluck of turkey-lackeys, and he busts a gut
At the wobblegobble dance one does without a head.

Tweet-tweet, meow-meow, Please sir, more porridge:
He alone, his grub growing hard, goes No! goes Now! goes
    Boom!

Half-cocked blacksmith, he lifts from hell's hottest forge
His latest law and with it brands a breast, a groin, a brain,

And like a pig farmer who's plucked a blackberry from a vine,
Savors the sweet spurt, before he turns back to his swine.

(NOVEMBER 1933)

This poem is known as "The Stalin Epigram." Mandelstam recited it to a number of
people, one of whom informed on him. It led to Mandelstam's first arrest, in 1934,
and to his subsequent exile and eventual death.

NOWHERE AIR

Like water trickling from the highest ice
Its bracing ache, its brain-shard sweetness,
Its nowhere air of utter now,

So my sigh has lost its source,
And I live by meanings I cannot comprehend,
For every instant I must taste the instant that I end.

(1933)

MEMORIES OF ANDREY BELY

Brainfire in the brow, acetylene eyes—
As if the world stretched out one fingerlength of fury

And touched you younger, stronger, free
From any unmagical judgment, immune to the sad time's lies.

.

Jade sage, unslappable itch, crack in this Crackerjack
    kingdom:
It sat uneasily on you, that crown of flop

They made you wear, tinklebell, tinklebell, living hell,
Full stop:

You were no one's wholly, and you were no one's fool.

.

Like a light snow on lightless Moscow, filthy beauty,
Incomprehensible clarity,

Or like a muddleduck gaggle of little Gogols you had to herd,
They stormed through you, your poems, word by whirling
    word . . .

Andrey Bely was an important Symbolist poet as well as a critic and novelist.

•

Creator, night crier, cowlicked pupil, cooler-than-thou
     undergrad,
Collector of space, doctor of bird,

Tinklebell!

•

Firstborn, first flung to the howling winds, hounded
     over ice
To skate the age, waking and making meanings as you
     moved . . .

It may be, friend, that simplicity itself is sick past saving.
Sometimes a death sentence must be sung.

•

The maker's aim, the bullet-thought, the noise of time
     trued to a line:
This is no cap gun for little boys.

It's not the inky reams, nor tightest rhymes:
What rescues is the news that burns the mind.

Like dragonflies above some stagnancy, untouching,
    clutching the weeds,
Posterity's thick pencils swarmed your corpse.

And we, too, who loved you, make our makeshift designs,
Asking forgiveness from every line.

•

Between you and this land a band of ice is born.
Lie quiet, friend, lie quiet and grow less, an even stricter
    straightness.

And let the coming young never profane this orphan
    space,
Nor ask what the livid brain learns of pain's clean void.

(JANUARY 10–11, 1934)

OCTETS

GO

I love the early apparition of the sails,
The whipcrack distance and the gasping try
As once, twice, and even the third chance fails—
Before there comes the righting sigh,

The sharp arcs and the greensweeping speed
Of the racing boats as space—eerily intent, magisterially idle—
Carves in a kind of drowse of power,
Like a child that never knew a cradle.

THIS WHISPER

Schubert shining off the sea; birdswirl of Mozart;
Goethe, whistling, unbewildering empty pathways;
Even Hamlet with his half-acts, holding himself apart—
All loved the crowd's pulse, lived by the crowded phrase.

Maybe this whisper was born before the man,
When leaves in treelessness went whirling by.
Maybe those to whom we consecrate our lives
Lived into truths they did not understand.

SIXTH SENSE

The tiny intelligence that is another way of knowing,
Or the third eye of the lizard that hazards day;
Cathedraled helix, cloistered cochlea,
All the small-talking antennae, touching, going—

How near it is, the nothing you can sense
Is everything, as if existence
Pressed a note into your grasping fingers,
Which you unfold and find blank, and now must answer.

EYE
Then the hard blue eye grew harder
Than the cold forms and fossils of nature,
And saw, inside that law of rock and bark, creatures
Crazed and crying cries of oil and ore.

And somewhere skin under skin the fetus kicks and kinks
Like a mile made of music, hairpin hornturns of a road
    headed home—
As if the forming brain became a thing space thinks,
Felt the promise of petal and the day of the dome.

(1932–1935)

VORONEZH NOTEBOOKS

(1934–1937)

BLACK CANDLE

Your girlish shoulders are for blushing,
For blushing under whips, and in dawn's raw ice to shine.

Your childlike hands are for pushing,
For pushing flatirons and feed sacks, and knotting twine.

Your feet, infant-tender, are for tiptoeing,
Tiptoeing through shattered glass, in the blood-tracked clay.

And I, I am for you, a black candle burning,
Like a black candle I am burning, and dare not pray.

(FEBRUARY 1934)

TICK

Street-creepers, sleep's assassins, power's parasites,
To you I send these souvenirs

Of exile's endless nights:
Painwire in the siren's whine,

Champagne proclamations undermined
By the lees of me.

How's the metro these days?
And the cherry buds—pretty?

Don't talk, spare your strength,
Hold hard to this hard city

And its wonky clocks,
Lists and twists enough to make one seasick,

And then, again,
All of space crushed suddenly to one dark tick.

(APRIL 1935)

BLACK EARTH

Earthcurds, wormdirt, worked to a rich tilth.
Everything air, star; everything earth.

Like a choir acquiring one clean sound—brief ringing
    kingdom—
These wet crumbs claim and proclaim my freedom.

A thousand plowed-up mounds exploding speech:
Infinite distance an infant's hand can reach—

All past blackness somehow, a blueness, a newness, a spell:
War here is a word, work a world in which to dwell.

Shit: earth's a botch, a bitch, blunt back of an ax:
Plea and eat dirt, bow down and be smashed.

Beware: the flute of rot lures and snares the ear,
The woodwind windbreak wakes an ache it cannot cure.

How sharp the plowshare, like a cutlass slashing fat.
How low, how clipped in April's upheaval, all the steppe lies
    flat.

Well . . . be well, black earth, be diligent, be visionary, be
    violent.
Oilvowels. Soilsayings. Silence.

(April 1935)

MANDELSTAM LANE

What the hell sort of street is this?
Mandelstam Lane.
Diabolical name!
Twist and twist
And it all comes out the same:
More kinked than the kinks in a madman's brain.

Well, a ruler he was not.
I'll say, and his morals hardly lily.
And that's why this street,
Or rut, really,
Or pit pickaxed to the tune of Goddamn!—
Goes by the name of Mandelstam.

(April 1935)

YOU HAVE STOLEN MY OCEAN

You have stolen my ocean, my swiftness, my soar,
Delivered me to the clutch of uprupturing earth,

And for what?
The mouth still moves though the man cannot.

(MAY 1935)

TODAY IS ALL BEAK

Today is all beak, little yellow hell
Pecking, pecking at my stone brain.

And the seaside dock gates, and the locked anchor chains,
Even the inchoate mist, see, somehow, me.

Black warships inching distance as through oil.
Black wakes like waves of sound that never sounded.

And here, between the boat slips, icy emaciations
Past blackness somehow, the color of plummet . . .

(DECEMBER 1936)

THE CAGE

When the goldfinch like a pop in sap
Angers up

From its man-made perch
To its slanderous plank;

And the light-silver lines in which no light
Is caught

Jingle and shake
Like a bear's bells

Then the world wears its nerves
And like a forest folds itself

Around a green untouchable interior
Only for a livewire, haywire little bird.

(DECEMBER 1936)

CONSIDER THE RIVER

Like a late gift long awaited, winter:
Personal, palpable stirrings.

I love the early animal of her,
These woozy, easy swings.

Soft atrocity, sweet fright,
As if for ravishment one first bowed and gave thanks . . .

And yet, before the forest's clean, hewn circle of light,
Even the raven banks.

Power more powerful for its precariousness,
Blue more blue for its ghost of white:

Consider the river, its constancy, its skin of almost ice,
Like a lullaby nullified by wakefulness . . .

(DECEMBER 29–30, 1936)

ALONE I LOOK INTO THE EYE OF ICE

Alone I look into the eye of ice.
It's going nowhere, which is my home.
And always the flat miraculous land breathing ceaseless,
Creaseless, ironed by what hand, smoothed under whose hum?

A wine-eyed sun, an air of laundered poverty,
Consoling by its sense of having been consoled.
Ten times ten times ten the trees . . . endlessly.
Eyesight like bootsteps, icelight like bread, innocent, bold . . .

(JANUARY 16, 1937)

STEPPES

Openness or emptiness, I'm sick of it:
Horizon everywhere,
Infinity forced down the gullet:
Eat your god, child, and love it!
To be blinded would be a mercy here.

Better to live alluvial,
Better to live layered downward,
To be a man of sand, of hollows, shallows,
To cling to sleeves of water
And to let them go—

An eon's tune, an instant's.
I might have rained the rapids back.
I might have learned to hear
In any random rotting log
A tree release its rings year by slow year.

(JANUARY 16, 1937)

SORROWDRAWL

Shut up: to be alone is to be alive,
To be alive to be a man—
Even hazied, even queasied by this madsmash hinterland,
Lost and locked in the sky's asylum eye.

This is my prayer to the air
To which I turn and turn expecting news or ease,
Nerves minnowing from shadowhands
Toward shadowlands inside of me. This is my prayer

To be of and under a human-scale sky,
To suffer a human-scale why, to leave
This blunt sun, these eternal furrows,
For the one country that comes when I close my eyes.

(JANUARY 18, 1937)

MOUNT ELBRUS

Spiderlight, sticky expectant dread:
I turn and turn, only more entangled
In today . . .

We need bread, and we need plain air,
But we need, too, some distant unbreathable peak,
Some eye-annihilating glare . . .

If the ache is nameless, how do I ask for ease?
If the I itself is exile, can the soul survive
Such private ice?

Old touchstone, to touch a stone, but in all that I have known,
Never, not once, such clear
Dreamweeping distillations of atmosphere . . .

We need poetry to wake the dark we are,
To find us and bind us beyond us
To an age of wakefulness

In the one day's unentangling sun,
Our breathing easy, ancient, like the pulse and peace
Of iambs counting down to silence.

(JANUARY 19, 1937)

Mount Elbrus is in the Caucasus Mountains. It is the highest mountain in Europe.

THE POEM

White meteorite, infinity's orphan, word
Painwaking particular earth . . .

Supplicants, tyrants, it doesn't matter.
It *is* matter: unbudgeable, unjudgeable, itself.

(JANUARY 20, 1937)

MOUNDS OF HUMAN HEADS

Mounds of human heads and mine
Among them, unseen, unmarked, unmourned.

But look: in lines as cherished as a lover's scars,
In screams of children who play at wars,

I rise with my hands of wind, my tongue of sun.

(1937)

ARMED WITH THE EYE OF THE ARROWING WASP

Armed with the eye of the arrowing wasp,
Plunging to the pith of urge, churn of earth,
I move by feel and smell among the simple given,
Gift by gift reciting now, scar by scar . . .

Yet here is no lasting image, no heaven coaxed from string,
And do not call this cry a song.
Little cut in life, rut in time, I long
For the sly start, the true inscrutable, mindrhyme, sleepsting.

Oh, to be made, marred, mired deep in time, to grasp,
When like a diver all of summer holds its breath
—Immune to miracles, deflecting death—
The very churn and urge, pith and earth . . .

(February 8, 1937)

ROUGH DRAFT

Provisionally, then, and secretive,
I speak a truth whose time is not:

It lives in love and the pain of love,
In sweat, and the sky's playful vacancy.

A whisper, then, a purgatorial prayer,
A testament of one man, in one place:

Our bright abyss is also—and simply—happiness,
And this expanding, life-demanding space
A lifetime home for us.

(MARCH 9, 1937)

MAYBE MADNESS

Maybe madness too has meaning here.
Maybe conscience, knotted like a cyst,
Knowing and being known by sun and air—
Maybe life unties and we exist.

Bring to mind the mindless spider, its care
For the pillared invisible, little crystal temple,
All air and otherness:

As if a form could thank its maker,
As if every line of light back to one source were drawn,
As if, deep in wilderness
A raftered hall rose around the risen guests,
All pains purged from their faces . . .

As it is on earth, Lord, not in heaven.
On earth, and in a house whose walls are song.
Even the birds, even the littlest, fearless.
O Lord, to live so long . . .

Forgive me this, forgive what I am saying.
Whisper it, less than whisper, like someone praying.

(MARCH 15, 1937)

FAITH

To taste in each leaf's sticky oath
The broken promise that is earth.

Mother of maple, mother of snow,
See how strong, how blind I grow,
Obeying rain, intuiting roots . . .

Frogs, all ooze and noise, bellvowel
Their bodies into a single aural oil.

Are these my eyes erupting green?
This my mouth mist seeks to mean?

Mother of maple, mother of snow . . .

(APRIL 30, 1937)

TO NATASHA SCHTEMPEL

As if to limp earth empty and to lift it up
With every hobbled heavened step;
As if to piece and place some delicate wreckage
Freely and fully in the space by which it's bound;
As if the halt in her were a halt of mind:
Three friends; laughter; landscape locked in time;
And the same gray weather mothering all to nothing
But the will to walk in a world made newly whole
Because the soul of brokenness is the soul.

(MAY 4, 1937)

Natasha Schtempel was a friend of the Mandelstams in Voronezh. She had a dis-
ability that affected her walk. Most American editions print this poem and the one
following as parts of a single poem. Russian editions vary quite a bit, however,
and as I was working on the poems they became, in my mind, separate from each
other.

THERE ARE WOMEN

There are women of budding blood, aboriginal earth.
Their steps are stifled cries.
Their calling is to ease the dead into being dead,
To walk calmly with the dead who rise.

There are women you can neither love nor leave.
They make your cravings criminal,
And eternal.

Today's angel, tomorrow's burrowing worm;
Time's intangibles, sorrow's color.

Here is one more step—halting, difficult, brave—
On this bloody beloved land.
Here is blank space where nothing, and no one, stand.

Flowers never wither. Heaven is whole.
It whispers what will be—
But not to me.

(MAY 4, 1937)

AND I WAS ALIVE

And I was alive in the blizzard of the blossoming pear,
Myself I stood in the storm of the bird-cherry tree.
It was all leaflife and starshower, unerring, self-shattering
    power,
And it was all aimed at me.

What is this dire delight flowering fleeing always earth?
What is being? What is truth?

Blossoms rupture and rapture the air,
All hover and hammer,
Time intensified and time intolerable, sweetness raveling rot.
It is now. It is not.

(MAY 4, 1937)

SECRET HEARING

On Translating Osip Mandelstam

Osip Mandelstam, one of the most serious and soul-demanding poets of the twentieth century, began as a whim for me. My wife was reading him, and sometime during our conversations I "translated" (I had no resources aside from other people's translations) a single early eight-line poem to try to show her something I could sense but could not find in any existing version. That poem isn't in this book (or in this world), but the failure sparked some latent interest and impulse in me, and the kindling caught. How, I wondered, could one voice contain such extremes of serenity and wildness, humor and horror? How could one man be so alive in the midst of so much death—including his always-impending own? How could such creedless cries seem as faithful as any saint's, such outright anguish like some new—and now essential—form of praise? As I said: soul-demanding.

When I have published these poems in magazines, or have read them at readings, I've been careful to call them versions and not translations, hoping to skip over the abyss of argument that opens underneath that distinction. Not because the argument isn't sometimes valid but because its lines are so clearly drawn by this point. Perhaps translations produced by people who don't speak the original language can never be worthy of that word. I'm hesitant to claim it for these poems, at any rate, though in the end the marketing department thought—rightly, no doubt—that the distinction would be lost on, and merely confusing to, a lot of potential readers.

As it happens, some of these poems *are* in fact quite close to their originals. Others are more like liberal transcriptions of original scores, and still others are more like collisions or collusions between (I hope!) Mandelstam and me, poems in the tradition of Alexander Pope's Homer, Robert Lowell's *Imitations*, Christopher Logue's Homer, et cetera. I couldn't say which approach comes closest to the essence of Mandelstam, but I can say that all were, in their various ways, aiming at that.

In any event, Mandelstam is a particularly difficult poet to translate. He seemed not to believe in the process himself (see "To the Translator") or to believe in it only in the most radical instances (see his own disfigured and essentially untraceable versions of Petrarch, or his scathing comments against translations that were "over-refined, excessively accurate, and academic"). He spoke often of the "secret hearing" essential to being a great poet, a quality I take to be analogous to T. S. Eliot's sense of the "auditory imagination," in which a poet hears rhythms before he has words for them. These rhythms are not simply an interior noise, some pulse of brain and blood—though they are that. No, they are *in* creation and not simply *of* it—"a thousand plowed-up mounds exploding speech"—and they are accessible, at first, only to the poet, and only to the poet who submits completely to his gift. There is an active element, to be sure. It takes ego to think the world needs one more poem, and needs it from you. It takes a saint not to feel some pride in the finished thing. But there is also in poetic creation an element of passivity, of givenness, without which everything is factitious dross, and any poet worth his salt knows in his bones how little he has had to do with his best poems.

Certainly Mandelstam knew it. You can feel him working his way toward this secret hearing in his early poems. (One doesn't "master" a gift like this; at best one attains the discipline of remaining vulnerable to it.) He was always a poet of high stylistic finish and formal control, but in the early poems, especially the most famous ones, like "Tristia" or "Hard Night," there is something tamped down, remote, withheld.* Of course, you might not even know this were it not for the later poems, particularly the poems from the *Voronezh Notebooks*, when he attains—at times is overwhelmed by—a seething, savage, Stravinskyan sort of music that is always testing, and teeming out of, its own angularities. These poems are formal and deformed, fluent and violent. It is as if the poet has been plugged right into the heart of existence, and the message by which he's electrified—Mandelstam composed entirely in his head, walked around Voronezh hum-

---

* "Cathedral, Empty" seems like an aberration from what I'm describing, but that's me, not Mandelstam. I couldn't leave this poem out, because it nagged at me so (it still does), but I couldn't make it work in English without radically reimagining it. The same is true of "You."

ming and mumbling to himself like a hymnist in hell—is, at its essence, music.

Previous translators, even when they've used rhyme and meter, have not tried to reproduce this music. Nor have I, since that would be impossible. But I have wanted to make poems that sing in English with something of Mandelstam's way of singing, poems that follow their sounds to their meanings, and that evince a formal imperative that is as strong as—indeed, is inextricable from—their emotional one. I have, in short, followed my own ear, as instinctively and obsessively as if I were writing my own poems, though it never felt like that, and these are not poems that I could ever write. For the poet, true inspiration is always a mixed experience, a sacred erasure of self for the sake of soul. The translator feels, at best, only the ghost of that god. The poet staggers around the streets of a little town in Russia, pursued by both death (Stalin) and life (poetry). The translator sits in North Chicago, sipping tea.

Well, I suppose the connection may be a bit sharper than that. I wrote all of these translations during an extended period of ill health. The details aren't important, except insofar as they left me with a lot of time to lie in bed and think. It is a truism to say that affliction can be a gift, and it is offensive to assert this from outside of any person's particular affliction. But still, pain can crack open whatever spiritual or psychological carapace has kept us from seeing or experiencing some things. Some kinds of art, for example. I was drawn to Mandelstam's work because of its urgency, but I was drawn into it—I have realized this only in retrospect—because of my own. "So my sigh has lost its source," he writes in "Nowhere Air":

And I live by meanings I cannot comprehend,
For every instant I must taste the instant that I end.

How deeply I respond to this poem—the way it articulates the peculiar despair that seeps into an imagination in which the well of futurity has been poisoned; the refreshing (and wise) anti–carpe diem quality of it; the sinuous lyric coherence that—if you listen closely, and as you read more of his work—begins to sound like a whole new species of hope.

And that is, finally, what one feels most deeply after living with Mandelstam for a while: the creative defiance; the unkillable capacity for wresting light out of darkness, or making darkness express itself lightly; the hope. He is a model not only for how to be a poet, but for how to be alive. How touching and wrenching it is to imagine him in those last, doomed days in Voronezh, still making his poems, still making them true to the wonderful, terrible reality around him, still astonished at consciousness, its gift, its cost:

Blossoms rupture and rapture the air,
All hover and hammer,
Time intensified and time intolerable, sweetness raveling rot.
It is now. It is not.

NOTES AND
ACKNOWLEDGMENTS

I couldn't have written this book without Ilya Kaminsky, who has given me word-by-word versions and transliterations of many of the poems, talked me through their textures and particularities, and been behind me—often ahead of me, actually—every step of the way. Ilya is a genius, of life as well as art, and his rollicking Russian enthusiasm for this project is what kept it alive.

I'm also grateful to Helena Lorman of Northwestern University, who provided me with additional trots, scholarly notes, and many explanations of word choices, idioms, and formal matters.

My process was to work with strict word-to-word versions, transliterations of the Russian so that I could get a sense of the sound and see where the rhymes were occurring, and all available translations. I often used critical and biographical material to gain insight into a particular poem. Kiril Taranovsky's book *Essays on Mandelstam*, Clare Cavanagh's *Osip Mandelstam and the Modernist Creation of Tradition*, and, of course,

Nadezhda Mandelstam's *Hope Against Hope* were all valuable in this regard. In the end, everything went back to Ilya for comment, and then I revised—not always *toward* the Russian original but toward the independent English mongrel that was emerging out of all these influences and inputs.

Aside from versions of individual poems by Robert Lowell, Stanley Kunitz, Donald Davie, and Joseph Brodsky, I am indebted to the translations of W. S. Merwin and Clarence Brown, Burton Raffel and Alla Burago, Richard and Elizabeth McKane, David McDuff, James Greene, Maria Enzensberger, David Tracy, and to the various translators in *Modernist Archaist: Selected Poems by Osip Mandelstam*.

Although my translations deviate radically from all previous versions of Mandelstam, I have in a couple of instances used phrases that seemed to me too perfect to ruin, or have adapted the phrasings of an individual line, or sometimes even a single word:

The title and first half of the first line of "Today Is All Beak" come from W. S. Merwin and Clarence Brown's version of that poem ("Today is all beak and no feathers").

In "Octets," the fourth line of "This Whisper" is an adaptation of Donald Davie's "All took the crowd's pulse, banked on the crowded phrase" from his version of the same poem.

In "The Cage," I owe the inspired "slanderous" to Richard and Elizabeth McKane.

One other debt: The sixth line of "Armed with the Eye of the Arrowing Wasp" is an adaptation of the title of one of Hayden Carruth's books, *If You Call This Cry a Song*.

Except for a few instances, the titles in this book are mine, not Mandelstam's. He tended not to use titles. My versions seemed to need them.

Finally, I'm grateful to the editors of the *American Scholar*, the *Atlantic Monthly*, the *Nation*, the *New Criterion*, *Occasional Religion*, *Poetry International*, *Salmagundi*, and *Spiritus* for publishing early versions of some of these poems.